W9-CLM-191

101 THINGS TO
SEE AND DO IN
IRELAND

101 THINGS TO
SEE AND DO IN
IRELAND

IAN HILL

CRESCENT BOOKS
NEW YORK • AVENEL, NEW JERSEY

Text: Ian Hill
Editor: Fleur Robertson
Editorial Assistance: Deirdre
            Rennison Kunz
Original Design Concept: Peter
            Bridgewater, Nigel Duffield
Design: Jill Coote
Picture Research: Irish Tourist Board
            (Bord Fáilte): Clive Brooks,
            Ralph Keeley, Dublin,
            Mark Rowlette, London
            Michael Diggin Photography:
            Michael Diggin
            Picturepoint: Ken Gibson
            Slide File: Carrie Foucesca
Photography: Irish Tourist Board,
            Michael Diggin Photography,
            Northern Irish Tourist Board,
            Picturepoint, Slide File
Maps: MicroMap Ltd
Production: Ruth Arthur,
            Sally Connolly, Neil Randles,
            Andrew Whitelaw
Director of Production: Gerald Hughes
Typesetting: Julie Smith

CLB 2939
© 1993 Colour Library Books Ltd,
Godalming, Surrey, England.
All rights reserved.
This 1993 edition published by
Crescent Books, distributed by
Outlet Book Company, Inc,
a Random House Company,
40 Engelhard Avenue, Avenel,
New Jersey 07001.
Printed and bound in Singapore.
ISBN 0 517 07306 4
8 7 6 5 4 3 2 1

Jacket: Muckross Lake, Co. Kerry, half title: Lough
Derg, Co. Tipperary and this page: St Finbarr's
Cathedral, Cork – all Michael Diggin Photography.
Title page: Co. Antrim glen, Picturepoint.

CONTENTS

INTRODUCTION

What country, least of all this green and pleasant isle, could be reduced to simply a collection of things to see and do? None, really, so this book is something like a device used by an illusionist. It will show you over 100 options and highlights but each, in its teasing way, will lead to dozens more, deftly revealed.

True, if you have but a limited amount of time, and wish to capture the essence of Ireland's beauty, these words and photographs will point you towards some of the very best Ireland has to offer, places which will turn you from the casual tourist into, hopefully, an entranced traveller. But if you set out to visit every one – be warned! – Ireland will have you in its thrall long before you have completed the task.

Ireland is an island situated off Europe, separated from Britain by the Irish Sea to its east. After its rugged west coast, the Atlantic has a straight run of some 2,000 miles to America. Though it is the size of Austria or the State of Maine, the island is home to a mere five million people. The six counties of Northern Ireland are part of the United Kingdom, the rest is a separate nation, the Republic of Ireland. The official

Dunluce Castle, County Antrim

language of the latter is Irish-Gaelic, a Celtic language that is spoken regularly by only some 55,000 people, most of whom live in the far west. The recognised second language is English, which is spoken by the majority.

Geographically Ireland is shaped rather like a saucer, consisting of a central plain surrounded by a rim of hills and mountains that fall into a coastline of sandy beaches, sheltered bays warmed by the Gulf Stream, and rugged cliffs. The Shannon and the other great fish-rich rivers wind lazily across the plain. Together, river, plain, mountains and shore offer some of the most unspoilt, unpolluted landscapes in Europe.

Yet, with or without these facts, few travellers lack images of Ireland before they arrive. The images come to mind with ease: green patchwork fields speckled with whitewashed cottages nestling under purple mountains; pubs full of men playing and looking like The Chieftains, the tables

Lough Gill, County Sligo

Cobh harbour, County Cork

in front of them dappled with rings from Guinness glasses; dappled trout rising to a mayfly; small girls with broad, freckled, smiling faces set in a glow of curly red hair; Maureen O'Hara and big John Wayne facing up in *The Quiet Man*; the beaches in *Ryan's Daughter*; James Joyce's wire-framed spectacles; Bing Crosby's voice crooning *Galway Bay*; a Claddagh ring given or received; the word Belfast coming from a television screen; Van Morrison; U2; Enya.

Ireland is, it can be guaranteed, very obliging. It will match those images like a mirror, but it will offer you something else too, something writers can but hint at, photographers only suggest. In Irish it is *craic* (pronounced 'crack'). *Craic* is the

Dublin pub

open friendliness of a quizzical joke as someone fills up your car with fuel, or banters as he takes your order in the restaurant, comments wryly on your fly cast or your golf swing, pours you a pint, or directs you back to the Cistercian abbey you lost between fuchsia hedges on a winding road. The Irish are probably the best talkers in the world and if you make time to listen, they have much to tell. For to the people who live on the island of Ireland, north and south, the history of their country is not just a rote of long-past dates, but a living reality, an integral part of daily life. Of local folk tales there are thousands, for scarcely a rock or a river, a village or a valley is without memory of past glory or grief. Poems, verse and anecdotes are to be heard on all sides and at almost all times. In the final analysis the greatest 'highlight' will be the Irish themselves.

Tread softly, and they'll tell you their dreams.

Cottage, County Laois

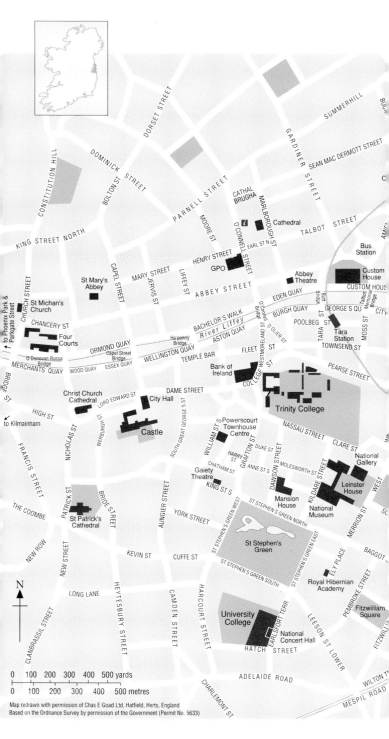

DUBLIN

Few cities can compete with Dublin as a traveller's destination. Large enough, cosmopolitan enough, to have all the airs of a European capital, it yet retains enough of a village feel to keep it essentially Irish.

The Guinness really does taste differently here and the brash property developers seem to have been stopped just in time before too many of the fine Georgian doorways and squares disappeared in the rush for another million pounds.

There are still secondhand bookshops to browse in by the River Liffey; and up on its right bank, just a few minutes walk from the city centre on the hills, the Norsemen raided in the ninth century. The early Christian churches, built by those who succeeded the Norsemen, are still standing.

Ptolemy, the Alexandrian geographer, mentioned Dublin in AD 140. He called it Eblana. St Patrick landed here in 448, the Danes in 840, taking for their base the south bank settlement of Dubh linn ('dark pool' in Irish). They quickly expanded on to the north bank but were expelled in 1014. Strongbow led the colonising Anglo-Normans here in the latter part of the 12th century, and Henry II granted the city a charter in 1171. Wars, reverses and counter reverses, continued for centuries, the English holding Dublin and the lands close to it known as the Pale. In its time an ecclesiastical settlement, a Viking trading post, a Norman stronghold and the second city of the British Empire, Dublin had a brief autonomy in the late 18th century, ended by the Act of Union.

The city declined in the 19th century into a shabby backwater familiar to readers of James Joyce. But it was restored as a capital city following the achievement of Irish independence in 1922. Property developers tried their best to destroy its Georgian glories in the boom days of the 1960s without quite succeeding and today the city rejoices in a distinctive continental atmosphere. Nominated at the start of the Nineties as a European City of Culture, the Irish capital enters the last decade of the century crowned by a thousand years of history, to take its rightful place among Europe's most elegant centres of power.

Four Courts

Age of Enlightenment

The 18th century was Dublin's, as architecture and the arts blossomed in a newly wealthy and confident metropolis.

- The Bank of Ireland was once the Parliament House (1733), the first custom-built parliament building in the world. The bank has guided tours.

- Probably the capital's most magnificent building, the Custom House stands on the Liffey downriver from O'Connell Bridge.

- See the Four Courts a mile upriver from the Custom House. The restored

General Post Office

dome is not a replica of the original and some think it too high. Do you?

- Dublin's most famous building, the 1818 General Post Office was where the 1916 Rising began. See the Proclamation of the Republic inside.

- One of the largest public parks in Europe, Phoenix Park was once an 18th-century duelling ground. Today it's the perfect place to unwind.

ADDRESSES **City maps & accommodation booking** Dublin Tourism, 14 Upper O'Connell St – Tel: (01) 747733. **Bank of Ireland** College Green, Mon-Fr 10am-12.30pm, 1.30-5pm. Guided tours Tue. **The Custom House** Custom House Quay. **The Four Courts** Inns Quay, Mon-Fr 9.30am-5pm. **The GPO** Lower O'Connell St, Mon-Sat 8am-8pm, Sun 10.30am-6.30pm.

Bank of Ireland

Custom House

St Patrick's Cathedral

God always joins Mammon, indeed usually preceeds him, in a city's fine stones, and thus it was with Dublin's. Close to the centre are some of the finest churches in Ireland.

- The River Poddle flows under St Patrick's Cathedral (1192), less than eight feet below the floor. Undaunted by such problems, it's the longest cathedral in the country.

- Another Anglican cathedral, Strongbow's Christ Church (1172) replaced Silkbeard's wooden church. Ask for the Archbishop's heart and the preserved cat and mouse.

- Marvel at the mummified bodies displayed in St Michan's (1095) near the organ that Handel played in 1742.

ADDRESSES **St Patrick's Cathedral** Patrick St, Mon-Fr 9am-6pm, Sat 9am-4pm. **Christ Church Cathedral** Christ Church Place, May-Sept Mon-Sat 9.30am-5pm; Oct-Apr Tue-Fr 9.30am-12.45pm & 2-5pm, Sat 9.30am-12.45pm. **St Michan's** Church St, Mar-Oct Mon-Fr 10am-5.30pm, Sat 10am-12.45pm, tours Nov-Mar – Tel: (01) 724154.

Christ Church Cathedral

Mummified bodies, St Michan's Church

DEAN SWIFT

*S*ee the grave of the great 18th-century Irish satirist Jonathan Swift, once Dean of St Patrick's, in the cathedral's nave. Swift wrote his own sharp epitaph: 'He is laid where bitter indignation can no longer rend his heart....'

Major Museums

These four museums are an indication of the variety of the capital's culture.

● The National Museum's Treasury in Kildare Street houses some of the finest early Irish relics in the land.

● The National Gallery of Ireland boasts Old Masters as well as Ireland's best. Take a morning here at least – there's a restaurant for the footsore.

● The Royal Hospital, Kilmainham's use for the Irish Museum of Modern Art shocked purists; judge for yourself.

● Kilmainham Gaol is now a museum. Inspect the cells of such as de Valera, later Ireland's president.

ADDRESSES **The National Museum** Kildare St, 10am-5pm weekdays, closed Mon, Sun 2-5pm – Tel: (01) 618811. **The National Gallery** Merrion Sq West, Mon-Sat 10am-6pm (9pm Thur), Sun 2-5pm – Tel: (01) 615133. **Irish Museum of Modern Art** Kilmainham, Tue-Sat 10am-5.30pm, Sun 12-5.30pm – Tel: (01) 718666. **Kilmainham Goal Museum** Kilmainham, July-Sept Wed & Sat 2-6pm; Oct-June Sun 2-6pm –Tel: (01) 535990.

Irish Museum of Modern Art

National Gallery

National Museum

Kilmainham Gaol

A page from the Book of Kells

Merrion Square

Laid out in 1762, Merrion Square is renowned for its Georgian elegance and famous homes.

- No. 1: home of Sir William and Lady Wilde, parents of Oscar.

- No. 82: W.B. Yeats' house when he was a senator of the Irish Free State.

- The beautifully designed central gardens are open to the public.

Merrion Square plaque

Trinity College

The first student arrived at Dublin's celebrated seat of learning in 1594, after Elizabeth I founded the university in 1591. Statues of two of the most famous alumni stand on College Green.

- See the illuminated manuscripts of the Book of Durrow, as well as those of 'the world's most beautiful book', the Book of Kells, in Trinity's Library.

ADDRESS **Trinity College Old Library** College Green, mid-Oct to mid-June Mon-Fr 9.30am-10pm, Sat 9.30am-1pm; mid-June to mid-Oct Mon-Fr 9.30am-5pm, Sat 9.30am-1pm. Closed last 2 weeks of July – Tel: (01) 772941.

> 66 *In Dublin's fair city,*
> *Where the girls are so pretty,*
> *I first set my eyes on*
> *Sweet Molly Malone.* 99

Georgian elegance

Dublin dusk

Night Venues

- The National Concert Hall provides a great setting for classical musicians, and jazz, folk and dance groups too.

- Once, riots greeted Synge and O'Casey in Yeats' 1904 Abbey Theatre. Rebuilt in 1966, today it's Ireland's national playhouse.

- For an evening of traditional music, try the bars The Merchant (off Merchant's Quay) and An Béal Bocht.

ADDRESSES **National Concert Hall** Earlsfort Terrace, an Events Listing is available every month from tourist offices and the NCH – Tel: (01) 711888. **Abbey Theatre** Abbey St, Mon-Sat 8pm – Tel: (01) 787222. **The Merchant** 12 Bridge St – Tel: (01) 793797. **An Béal Bocht** Charlemont St – Tel: (01) 755614.

The Cup that Cheers

Mulligan's in Poolbeg Street, where, for the correct viscocity, they start pouring pints long before you order them, is one of the pubs in Joyce's *Ulysses*. Pubs are as much a part of Irish life as churches.

Mulligan's pub

- Theatrical pubs include Neary's, Chatham St, and McDaid's, Harry St, while writers find good company at Doheny & Nesbitt's, Baggot St, and Kehoe's, South Anne St.

- Live music can be found every night at The Brazen Head. The capital's oldest pub, it's rich with history.

- The non-alcoholic alternative: coffee and sticky buns in Bewley's Oriental Cafés – a great Dublin tradition.

ADDRESSES **The Brazen Head** 20 Bridge St – Tel: (01) 779549. **Bewley's Coffee Houses** Grafton St, Westmoreland St & South Great George's St, Mon-Sat 7.30am-6pm.

An Abbey Theatre production

Bewley's Oriental Café

Dublin's oldest pub

Where the writers go

Ryan's pub

THE NORTHWEST

THE NORTHEAST

Cavan

CAVAN

Lough
Sheelin

Longford

LONGFORD

THE
WEST

Lough
Ree

Athlone

L Owel

L Ennell

WESTMEATH

Mullingar

Tullamore

OFFALY

Birr

Slieve
Bloom Mts

Port Laoise

Roscrea

LAOIS

R Nore

Kildare

KILDARE

The Curragh

LEINSTER

Cooley
Mts

Dundalk

LOUTH

Ardee

Mellifont Abbey
Newgrange

Monasterboice

Drogheda

Kells

Navan

MEATH

Hill of
Tara

R Boyne

Dunshaughlin

DUBLIN

IR
S

Straffan

Enniskerry

Bray

Wicklow
Mts

Great Suga

Glendalough

Ash

WICKLOW

Wic

Avoca

Arklow

Carlow

CARLOW

R Barrow

Mt
Leinster

Kilkenny

KILKENNY

THE SOUTH

N

Jerpoint
Abbey

Blackstars
Mts

Enniscorthy

WEXFORD

Ferrycarrig

Wexford Slobs

New Ross

Wexford

Rosslare

R Suir

Fethard

Kilmore
Quay

Hook Head
Lighthouse

ST GEORGE'S CHA

Motorway
Main road
Other road
Railway
Towns
Places of Interest
Mountain

0   10   20 miles
0   10   20   30 km

Based on the Ordnance Survey by permission of the Government (Permi

THE
DUBLIN REGION

The old province of Leinster stretched out from Dublin, south over the hills of Wicklow, through Wexford to the River Suir flowing into Waterford's great natural harbour. North again, the gentle counties of Kilkenny, Carlow, then Laois and Offaly join with Kildare, the River Liffey's county. Northwest, the River Shannon forms a natural boundary, cutting off Meath, Westmeath and Longford and the lake-strewn border counties of Leitrim, Cavan, Monaghan and Louth from the wilder west.

This province included both the counties of the Pale, where English colonial rule held sway, and others that extended beyond it. Inside the old Pale, town patterns are tidy and circumspect, often being based on old, defensible military plans. Just outside, castles and forts range everywhere – evidence of the colonists' need for security. Further west, town plans relax, even sprawl. The military had no part in their planning.

But Leinster's heritage is older than colonial times. Tara, the Hill of the High Kings of Ireland, now bare of all but a brooding presence, is here in Meath. In the fertile Boyne Valley rest the great passage graves of Dowth, Knowth and Newgrange that pre-date the Egyptian pyramids. They are evidence of a flourishing 3,000 B.C. civilisation, the most advanced in the Europe of its time, and now each one is an essential for visitors. All three offer tantalising clues to this lost, mysterious civilisation. Cuchulainn, Ulster's hero, fought his ledgendary battles in Louth's Cooley Mountains. Further south, early Celtic Christianity flourished for many years in the great monastic settlements of Glendalough, Jerpoint, Monasterboice and Kells.

The Boyne Valley has witnessed much and memories are long. St Patrick first proclaimed Christianity by lighting a fire on the Hill of Slane in County Meath, thereby challenging the druids for whom the hill was sacred. In the mid-17th century Cromwell massacred the inhabitants of nearby Drogheda during his 'subduing' of Ireland and his name is still accursed there to this day. Equally dramatically, Protestant William III won the Battle of the Boyne here against Catholic James II in 1690, an outcome that still has significance in the North.

Yet, for all that, this is largely lush and peaceful farming region. County Wicklow is nicknamed the 'Garden of Ireland', but that is a title that could genuinely be applied to many of these counties of the Pale. Relaxed and rural, yet never far from Dublin, this region's attractions are some of the country's brightest and best.

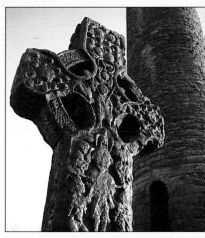

South Cross, Kells

Wanderings in Wicklow

Take time to enjoy the best of this warm and relaxing county, so close to Dublin.

● Follow the old pilgrim route through the Wicklow Gap to see Glendalough, a once-great 6th-century monastery.

● See the immaculate landscaped gardens of fire-gutted Powerscourt House, plus Ireland's highest waterfall, a deer herd and fine views.

● Dally in Mount Usher, one of the finest gardens in Ireland, and take tea or a drink afterwards in the nearby old coaching inn, Hunter's Hotel.

Glendalough Round Tower

Powerscourt House

● Visit the Meeting of the Waters in Avoca, and see Avondale, the home of the Irish patriot Parnell (1846-91).

● Climb the Sugar Loaf mountain near Kilmacanogue. The ascent is easy and on a clear day you can see all the way to Wales.

ADDRESSES **Glendalough Monastery** Laragh, Nov to mid-Mar Tue-Sun 10am-4.30pm; mid-Mar to June, mid-Sept to end Oct daily 10am-5pm; mid-June to mid-Sept daily 10am-7pm – Tel: (0404) **45325. Powerscourt Gardens** Enniskerry, Mar-Oct 9am-5.30pm, waterfall all year 10.30am-7pm or dusk – Tel: (01) 2867676. **Mount Usher Gardens** Ashford, mid-Mar to Oct Mon-Sat 10.30am-5.30pm, Sun 11am-5.20pm – Tel: (0404) 40116. **Hunter's Hotel** Rathnew – Tel: (0404) 40106.

Mount Usher Gardens

Wexford Waders and Wraiths

- Rare Greenland white-fronted geese wait in winter for birdlovers on the Wexford Wildfowl Reserve, as do waders all year.

- Don't miss the beauty spots of Mount Leinster in the Blackstairs Mountains or Kilmore Quay at Forlorn Point.

- The Irish National Heritage Park portrays Irish life through the ages. Great views of the Slaney Estuary.

- Try a hand of bezique with Miss Tottenham at Fethard's Loftus Hall Hotel. The Devil sat across the baize from her in 1750. Her ghost comes back for more.

Kilmore Quay

Thatcher, Irish National Heritage Park

ADDRESSES **Wexford Wildfowl Reserve** Wexford Slobs, Visitor Centre open daily 9am-sunset – Tel: (053) 23129. **Irish National Heritage Park** Ferrycarrig, daily Mar-Oct 10am-7pm – Tel: (053) 23406. **Loftus Hall Hotel** – Tel: (051) 97154.

Tern

Wexford Slobs

Kilkenny and Kildare

For medieval history and million-dollar horses try these counties of the Pale.

● Visit Kilkenny's Castle (1192) and grounds, now a National Historic Park, in one of the best-preserved medieval towns in the land. Don't miss the Kilkenny Design Centre.

● Further south, Jerpoint Abbey (1158) boasts fine stone carvings.

● Stop at Tully, near Kildare, to see the stallions of the National Stud. Don't miss the Curragh, Ireland's racing headquarters.

ADDRESSES **Kilkenny Tourist Office** Rose Inn St – Tel: (056) 21755. **Kilkenny Castle** Apr-May daily 10am-5pm; June-Sept 10am-7pm; Nov-Mar Tue-Sat 10.30am-12.45pm & 2-5pm, Sun 11am-12.45pm & 2-5pm. **Kilkenny Design Workshops** Castle St, normal shopping hours. **Jerpoint Abbey** Thomastown, mid-June to mid-Sept 10am-6pm daily; May to mid-June Tue-Sat 10am-1pm & 2-5pm, Sun 2-5pm – Tel: (056) 24623. **The National Stud** Easter Sun-Oct Mon-Fr 10.30am-5pm, Sat & Bank Hol 10.30am-6pm, Sun 2-6pm – Tel: (045) 21251. **Straffan Steam Museum** nr Celbridge, Co. Kildare, Sun & Bank Hol ex 24 Dec-2 Jan, daily July & Aug 11.30am-5.30pm – Tel: (01) 628 8412.

Thoroughbred mare and foal

Kilkenny Castle

Ancient Meath and Louth

These counties of the Pale boast historic remains dating from the earliest times to the 19th century. Sample the past.

● High Crosses told biblical strip cartoons. Those in Monasterboice, County Louth, and Kells, County Meath, had superb artist-masons.

STRONG STEAM

*L*overs of steam should see Richard Trevithick's Third Model of 1797 – the oldest surviving self-propelled object in existence – at the Steam Museum in Lodge Park, Straffan, Co. Kildare.

Muiredach's Cross, Monasterboice

ADDRESSES **Mellifont Abbey** Collon,
nr Drogheda, May to mid-June Tue-Sat
9.30am-5.30pm, Sun 2-5.30pm; mid-
June to Sept daily 10am-6.30pm – Tel:
(041) 26459. **Dunsany Castle** near
Dunshaughlin, May-July Mon-Sat 9am-
1pm with guided tours at 9am, 10am,
11am & noon – Tel: (046) 25198.
Newgrange Tumulus southeast of
Slane, Co. Meath, daily mid-Mar to May
10am-1pm & 2-5pm; daily June to mid-
Sept 10am-7pm, last tour at 6.30pm;
daily mid-Sept to Oct 10am-1pm & 2-
5pm; Nov to mid-Mar Tue-Sun as above
but closes at 4.30pm – Tel: (041) 24488.

- Once a Cistercian monastery
suppressed by Henry VIII, then a
pigsty, then William III's Battle of the
Boyne headquarters, Louth's Mellifont
Abbey stones are quiet now.

- Lord Dunsany reared geese for quills
with which to write his poems. His
12th-century castle welcomes
visitors. See the Hill of Tara, once the
capital of Celtic Ireland, nearby.

- The finest passage grave in Europe,
Newgrange was built 4,000 years
ago. Eerie at the winter solstice, the
one time the sun shines all along the
tomb passage.

Mellifont Abbey

Newgrange tomb passage

Hill of Tara

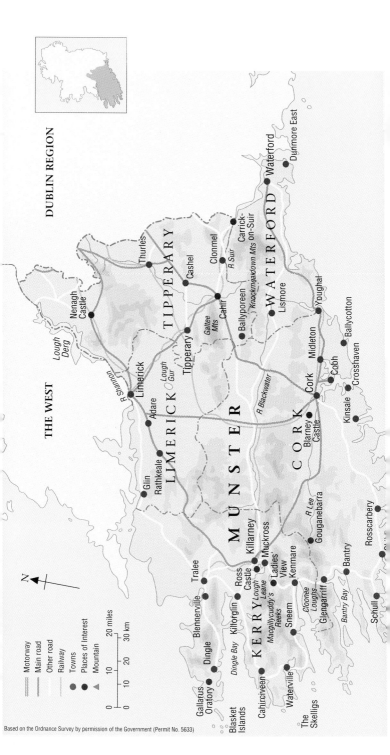

THE
SOUTH

The little towns of the South never seem old. But for the Georgian courthouse and the Protestant church, in the shadow of some gaunt, ruined abbey, nothing in them predates the 19th century. A windowless mill or an ivy-covered riverside warehouse attest to a once-flourishing linen trade devastated by cheap cotton imports. A central square of buildings has grown up round a fair-day space for enclosing animals. Fine shop fronts with gilt signs distinguish the long-established family firms. Beyond the square, buildings straggle the county roads in ever-diminishing numbers. Beer-brown water flows under a stone bridge. The pace of life is slow and relaxing, the atmosphere welcoming, the weather 'soft'.

West of the deep harbours of the south coast, where the clippers landed tea and cotton and took on cattle and butter, and beyond the smaller inlets, where pirates once huddled and caroused, waiting intelligence of a heavily laden West-Indiaman, the Atlantic crashes dramatically on rocky shores. Here in Kerry ring forts and strong castles show that the cattle farmers were prepared to defend their riches from the Vikings. But forts fell to iron and to bronze; great clan castles, once impregnable, were defeated by gunpowder. At sea, rich rafts of plankton brought the herring and the pilchards which first tempted the Iberian fishermen – a trade still in evidence in the ports now.

In the broader valleys the English travellers settled, attracted by the salmon-rich rivers and the Mediterranean-like micro-climate that allowed fine produce and exotic shrubs to flourish in the gardens of the grand. Nurtured by this climate of warmth and water, this has always been a most picturesque region. Waterford is typical in its many kinds of beauty, much of the north and centre of the county being mountainous, the rest consisting of gentle hills and valleys. Cork, the largest county in Ireland, also has its share of lovely river valleys, as well as some of the best coastal scenery in the land, especially the farther southwest you travel. All along the coast, restaurants boast fine seafood, and the great city of Cork itself has a distinctly continental air. But, arguably, the loveliest of all is Kerry, in the extreme southwest. Renowned the world over for its unspoilt beauty, no visitor to Ireland should miss this county's wooded shores and glens, its lakes sprinkled with lonely islands and embraced by the country's highest mountains. Indeed, rain or shine, the South is surely the most dazzling jewel in Ireland's crown.

Dingle Peninsula, County Kerry

Waterford Way

It was Vadrefjord when the Danes built the city walls and Reginald's Tower, but it stood an English colony until the 19th century. Now, Waterford means glass.

● Royal residence, mint, ordnance, jail – Reginald's Tower of 1003, now a civic museum, welcomes you to its scarred walls.

● Building on standards the Penrose brothers set in 1783, today's Waterford Glass blowers and cutters amaze. Don't miss them.

ADDRESSES **Waterford Heritage Centre** Greyfriars St, Easter-Oct Mon-Fr 9.30am-5.30pm, Sat 10am-2pm. **Waterford Tourist Office** 41 Merchant's Quay, May-Sept Mon-Sat 9am-6pm; Oct-Apr Mon-Fr 9am-12.45pm & 2-5.15pm – Tel: (051) 75823. **Reginald's Tower** Easter-Sept 11am-1pm & 2-4pm, Sat 11am-1pm. **Waterford Crystal Glass** Kilbarry, tours (must book) Mon-Fr 10am-2.30pm – Tel: (051) 73311.

Reginald's Tower, Waterford

Waterford Glass worker

River Runs

The south coast's big, safe-haven harbours and lush river valleys provide temptations for those who only wish to stand and stare, listening to the wind.

● Cruise, one way or both, down the River Suir and up the Barrow across to Wexford's medieval New Ross.

● England's Crystal Palace's designer, Joseph Paxton, designed Lismore Castle to dominate the Blackwater's ever-so-English-looking river valley.

● Lunch *al fresco* watching boats bob in Dunmore East's attractive port at the mouth of Waterford Harbour, estuary of the Suir and Barrow rivers.

Lismore Castle

Game fishing on the River Suir

Dunmore East

Dunmore East

ADDRESSES **Galley River Cruises**
June-Aug – Tel: (051) 21723. **Lismore
Castle** (gardens only) May to mid-Sept
2.45-4.45pm ex Sat.

East Cork

- Fota Island in Cork Harbour has a
  superb arboretum.

- Sir Francis Drake, the great
  Elizabethan sailor, dodged Spaniards
  in Drake's Pool, Crosshaven, across
  the sound from Cobh's great harbour.

- Head east, past pretty Ballycotton, to
  Youghal, to view the Elizabethan
  mansion Myrtle Grove, where Raleigh
  is said to have first smoked tobacco
  and grown Ireland's first potatoes.

Fota Estate

ADDRESSES **Fota Island Arboretum**
Easter-Oct Mon-Sat 10am-5.15pm, Sun
11am-5.15pm – Tel: (021) 276871.
Myrtle Grove Youghal, 2 guided tours a
day in June, (3pm, 4.30pm) 3 a day in
July & Aug (11.45am, 3pm, 4.30pm) –
Tel: (024) 92274.

Cork City

Second city first, say the independently minded Corkonians who, from their 6th-century beginnings on the River Lee's once marshy banks, successfully absorbed both Dane and Norman and built the Republic's second largest city.

- Wander down to the restored Butter Market Shandon Craft Centre.

- St Patrick's Hill has the best panorama of the city.

- View works of art at the Crawford Art Gallery and enjoy its pleasant restaurant too.

- The best city walk is west along the tree-lined Mardyke, past the cricket ground and Fitzgerald Park to Cork's University College.

Grace Cup, Cork Public Museum

- Cork Public Museum in Fitzgerald Park has fine displays of silver and glass. Call in for a Garryduff Bird ring.

- See the rose window in St Finbarr's Cathedral, built in the 1870s on the site of the saint's 6th-century monastery.

- Cork Opera House hosts a great variety of entertainment from opera and ballet, to plays and musicals.

- Dan Lowrey's pub in MacCurtain Street is one of the city's best.

ADDRESSES **Tourist Information** Grand Parade – Tel: (021) 273251. **Shandon Craft Centre** Mon-Fr 9am-

University College, Cork

River Lee, Cork city

THE BELLS OF ST ANNE'S

Partly coloured like the people, red and white is Shandon's steeple, runs the jingle about St Anne's, where there are eight bells you can ring for a score of francs or a couple of dollars.

5.30pm. **St Ann Shandon Church** tower Mon-Sat 10am-4pm – Tel: (021) 501672. **Crawford Municipal Art Gallery** Emmet Place, Mon-Sat 10am-5pm – Tel: (021) 273377. **St Finbarr's Cathedral** Bishop St. **Cork Public Museum** Mon-Fr & Sun afternoons – Tel: (021) 270679. **Cork Opera House** Emmet Place – Tel: (021) 270022.

West Cork

A playground for locals, tourists and an increasing international community drawn by its position at the edge of the Old World, West Cork blends history, pretty towns, three varieties of stout and fine cooking in a potent mix.

- Kiss the stone named for Lord Blarney, who smooth-tongued his way round Elizabeth's court, and maybe share his eloquence.

- Dutch-gabled and hung with flower baskets, Kinsale's fabled restaurants specialise in the best seafood. After a good meal, examine star-shaped Charles Fort, Ireland's most massive fortification, nearby.

- See the lake they call Gouganebarra near Macroom and view St Finbarr's wonderfully situated Oratory.

St Finbarr's Oratory, Gouganebarra

Garinish Island

- Bantry House and its Italianate gardens should not be missed.

- Like Fota, famous Garinish Island in Glengarriff's harbour also has an astonishing arboretum. Glengarriff village lies in a breathtaking glen.

ADDRESSES **Blarney Stone, Blarney Castle** Mon-Sat 12.30-5.30pm, Sun 9.30am-5.30pm & **Blarney House & Gardens** June-Sept Mon-Sat 12.30-5.30pm – Tel: (021) 385252. **Charles Fort** mid-Apr to mid-June Tue-Sat 9am-5pm, Sun 2-5pm; mid-June to mid-Sept daily 10am-6.30pm – Tel: (021) 772263. **Bantry House & Gardens** Nov-Mar 9am-6pm; Apr-Oct dawn-dusk, interior Apr-Oct 9am-8pm – Tel: (027) 50047. **Garinish Island** Mar-June & Sept-Oct Mon-Sat 10am-6pm, Sun 1-6pm; July-Aug Mon-Sat 9.30am-6pm, Sun 11am-6pm.

Blarney Castle

Killarney's Lakes

Three wooded lakes lie east of Macgillycuddy's Reeks. France has the Eiffel Tower, India the Taj Mahal – Ireland has Killarney's lakes. Be prepared to surrender your individuality when confronted by this, some of the most beautiful scenery in the land.

Kate Kearney's Cottage

● Take the day-long trip: a jaunting car from your Killarney hotel door to Kate Kearney's cottage, then on through the dazzling Gap of Dunloe between Purple Mountain and Macgillycuddy's Reeks. Return by boat.

● Try the bateau-mouche from Ross Castle on the Lower Lake, or ask a boatman to row you out in style.

● Jaunt to Muckross House, for a fine tea, and azaleas in springtime.

● The Kenmare road from Killarney takes you to Ladies' View, one of the best. After Kenmare, see the beautiful Cloonee Loughs.

ADDRESSES **Killarney Tourist Office** Town Hall – Tel: (064) 31633. ***The Pride of Killarney* cruise boat** – Tel: (064) 32638. **Boat hire** – Tel: (064) 32252. **Muckross House, Killarney National Park** Mar-June & Sept-Feb 9am-6pm; July-Aug 9am-7pm – Tel: (064) 31440.

Gap of Dunloe

Cloonee Lough

Muckross House

A U T H O R ' S   T I P

Walk or bike the lakes in the evening, when sweating horses and perspiring tourists have gone home.

Ross Castle

Cahirciveen Bay

The Ring of Kerry

Surfeited with Killarney's charms? Move on: take the famous Ring of Kerry drive, a roller-coaster route around Iveragh's peninsula, hugging mountainside, sandy cove and glassy lake.

Sneem

- In pretty Sneem, the weather vane, in the form of a salmon, on the church reminds anglers to wet their lines in the rushing rivers hereabouts.

- In Cahirciveen, the Ring's capital, they'll tell you the ruined police barracks were built to plans intended for India's Northwest Frontier – looking at the scale of the remains, you can believe it, too.

- The Skellig Islands lie offshore. Monks once confronted the elements here. See what they had to endure....

- Waterville, favourite resort of Charlie Chaplin and George Bernard Shaw, might be yours too.

Great Skellig Island

Beauties and the Beast

The 'beautiful vale of Tralee' is the gateway to the Dingle Peninsula. Tralee itself boasts one of the most elegant Georgian thoroughfares in Ireland – and the Rose of Tralee beauty contest.

- See the town's imaginatively recreated medieval Irish community known as Geraldine Tralee.

- The sails of the island's only commercially run windmill turn at Blennerville on the shore of the Lee.

Kerry standing stone

Blennerville Windmill

Geraldine Tralee, Ashe Memorial Hall

- Fungi the dolphin entertains swimmers and divers in Dingle Bay.

- Find peace at Gallarus' stone Oratory, amongst beehive huts and standing stones scattered across Dingle's wild peninsula.

ADDRESSES **Rose of Tralee International Festival** late Aug – Tel: (066) 31322. **Geraldine Tralee** Ash Memorial Hall Apr-June Mon-Sat 10am-6pm; July-Aug Mon-Sat 10am-8pm; Sept-Nov as Apr-June; Apr-Nov Sun 2-6pm. **Blennerville Windmill** Blennerville, Apr-Oct daily 9am-6pm – Tel: (066) 21064. **Dingle Tourist Office** Main St (June-Sept) – Tel: (066) 51188.

Gallarus Oratory

❝ *Oh no, t'was not her beauty*
alone that won me,
T'was the truth in her
eyes ever dawning
That made me love Mary,
the Rose of Tralee. **❞**

Clogher Strand, Dingle Peninsula

Scarteen Black and Tan Hunt

Tipperary Travels

As sporting a county as ever you'll find.

● Archbishop Croke put up the money to found the Gaelic Athletic Association. You'll find hurling and his statue in Thurles.

● Capital of Ireland's greyhound racing, Clonmel has three handsome dogs on its coat of arms, a famous track and regular race nights.

ADDRESSES **Tipperary Tourist Office** – Tel: (062) 51457. **Clonmel Greyhound Stadium** Mon & Thur evng.

A KINGDOM FOR A HORSE

*ℋ*ire a hunter from a local riding school and during the season ride with the Scarteen Hunt, known as the 'Black and Tans'. With some of the best hunting country in the world, the hunts here welcome brave riders.

The Devil's Teeth

The Devil, they say, dropped a rock he'd bitten (Devil's Bit Mountain, Templemore) when, flying over Cashel, County Tipperary, he saw St Patrick building a church. Hence the Rock of Cashel.

- Fairytale in the distance, Cashel's turrets are just as magical close up.

- Cahir, Carrick, Nenagh – these are just some of the castles for your tour of Tipperary's 'Golden Vale' – the name deriving from Golden village.

- On June 3, 1984, Ronald Reagan visited Ballyporeen, checking where his great-grandfather came from.

ADDRESSES **Cashel Museum & Rock** June-Sept 9am-6pm; Oct-May 10am-5pm, Rock often later, & Nov-Feb till 4.30pm, tours – Tel: (062) 61437. **Cahir Castle** May to mid-June 10am-6pm; mid-June to Sept 10am-7.30pm; Oct-Apr ex Mon 10am-4.30pm – Tel: (052) 41011. **Nenagh Heritage Centre** mid-Apr to Nov Mon-Fr 10am-5pm, Sat & Sun 2.30-5pm – Tel: (067) 32633. **Ormonde Castle** Carrick-on-Suir, mid-June to Sept 10am-5.30pm, tours poss. – Tel: (051) 40787.

Ballyporeen

Nenagh Castle

Rock of Cashel

Limerick Strongholds

'It was an ancient city, well versed in the arts of war.' Thus wrote Virgil, of Troy. The same may be said of Limerick: town and county are both rich in fortifications.

- The bold towers of King John's Castle squat by Shannon's ford, where the Vikings, Normans, Cromwellians and Williamites fought in turn.

- Thatch tops whitewashed cottages in Adare, southwest of Limerick. Find the lichen-splashed ruins of the Franciscan Friary and Desmond Castle in Adare Manor's grounds.

- Gerald, Earl of Desmond, canters in legend on a silver-shod stallion across Lough Gur. Around the lake are Stone Age and Iron Age tombs, forts and lakeside dwellings.

King John's Castle

- South of Limerick, castles are everywhere. Take your pick from Matrix, Glin and many more.

ADDRESSES **Limerick Tourist Information** Arthur's Quay – Tel: (061) 317522. **Adare Manor Hotel** – Tel: (061) 396566. **Lough Gur** Visitor Centre May-Sept daily 10am-6pm – Tel: (061) 85186. **King John's Castle** 9.30am-5.30pm, variable winter – Tel: (061) 361551. **Castle Matrix** Rathkeale, May-Sept, Sat-Tue 1-5pm, all other times, tours by appointment – Tel: (069) 64284. **Glin Castle** Glin, May daily 10am-noon, 2-4pm, all other times, tours by appointment – Tel: (068) 34173.

Lough Gur Stone Circle

Castle Matrix

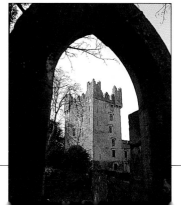

Adare Manor Hotel

ATLANTIC OCEAN

Erris Head

THE NORTHWES

Ballina

Lough Conn

R Moy

MAYO

Achill Is
Dooagh Bay

Carrowbeg

Castlebar

Boyle

Clew Bay
Westport Bay

Clare Is

Westport

ROSCOMMON

Louisburgh

Claremorris

Tulsk

Croagh Patrick

CONNACHT

Roscommon

Inishbofin Is

Killary Harbour

Kylemore Abbey

Lough Mask

Lough Ree

Cleggan

Connemara National Park

Cong

Tuam

Clifden

Twelve Pins

Lough Corrib

Connemara

Athlone

Ballyconneely

Roundstone

GALWAY

TH
DUB
REGI

Spiddal Galway

Ballinasloe

Rossaveel

Galway Bay

R Shannon

Dún Aengus

Kilronan

Ballyvaughan

Inishmore Is

Aillwee Caves

Gort

Aran Islands *Doolin Pt*

The Burren

Poulnabrone
Dolmen

Lough Derg

Cliffs of Moher

Liscannor

CLARE

Craggaunowen
Castle

Inagh

Ennis

Clare

Knappogue
Castle

R Fergus

Bunratty
Castle

Kilkee

N

Loop Head

THE SOUTH

≈≈≈≈ Motorway
▬▬▬ Main road
      Other road
- - - Railway
● Towns
● Places of Interest
▲ Mountain

0   10   20 mile
0   10   20   30 km

Based on the Ordnance Survey by permission of the Government (Permit No. 5633)

THE WEST

Once isolated between the broad Shannon and the storm-tossed Atlantic, Clare, Galway, Mayo and Roscommon, the counties of the West, were left alone by marauders and colonists. The bare, beautiful mountains, the ever-present mists, the seemingly endless bogs and the rock-strewn pastures, were a poor prize for the few who ventured that far. True, there is good land along the Shannon, but further west two cows can be called a herd and a field which sustains four a rare occurrence. The Vikings made few forays, the Norman tactic (and later Cromwell's) was more to drive the Irish west rather than settle there themselves.

Elizabethan planters and those who came after them never felt sure of their ground. An uncertain, isolated ascendancy went native, the big houses crumbling. In some landowners the isolation led to fear, panic and cruelty. And then there was the famine, the Great Hunger of the 1840s. Thousands sailed for America, sending money home if they could, and the tide of emigration has not entirely stopped even today. The ruined cottages – a burst of fuchsia or veronica by some tumbledown stones – stand for hardships not yet forgotten. Hardships remembered now in songs of deprivation, lost love and fierce defiance sung in the 'singing pubs' in Clare and in 'sessions' by Galway's quays.

In this bare landscape Christianity was also stripped down to essentials. Abbeys were small, the seeds of a tradition of asceticism were sown and grew, and nowhere more so than on the islands off the western coast where conditions were even harder. Tourists have brought a new prosperity to the west, tourists who, perhaps like the ascendancy before them, are capable of going a little native. Some come specifically for the lunar landscape of the flower-speckled Burren, the majesty of Croagh Patrick, or simply to buy a Claddagh ring or a length of handwoven, organically dyed tweed or a hand-knitted wool sweater from the place where they originated. Others seek the spiritual isolation of the island hermitages, the sight of a single donkey, creels loaded with turf, on a winding track under a wide sky in empty Connacht. Whichever or whatever it is, the West's welcome is always warm, the aroma of a turf fire close by. Park the car by a stream and wind down the window.

That's what you came for.

Clew Bay, County Mayo

Past Time's Pastimes

Once the fortresses of the warring MacNamara and O'Brien clans, the castles that dot the land between Slieve Bernagh and the Shannon now welcome visitors to revel in their rose-tinted pasts.

- Bunratty and Knappogue castles host medieval feasts; Knappogue's lauds Ireland's women in song and legend. Bunratty's has a Folk Park.

- Craggaunowen Castle takes you yet further back. View the Craggaunowen Project's recreations of Iron-Age life and the *Irish* discovery of America.

- The Burren's Aillwee Caves, still measureless to man, are two million years old. Tour stalactite and

Poulnabrone Dolmen

stalagmite, see where the bear slept and *feel* the dark when they turn out the lights....

- Poulnabrone Dolmen – an ancient burial chamber– lies 4 miles south of the Aillwee Caves on the Burren. It is Ireland's most photographed tomb.

- See how the poet Yeats roughed it in 16th-century Thoor Ballylee. See too Coole Park, once the demesne of the literary hostess Lady Gregory and now known for the Autographed Tree. Its bark bears the initials of many famous Irish writers.

- Don't miss the Cliffs of Moher, Europe's moodiest, near Liscannor.

Medieval feasting at Bunratty Castle

ADDRESSES **Knappogue Castle** southeast of Ennis, May-Oct 9.30am-5pm – Tel: (061) 71103, dinners by arrangement. **Bunratty Castle Folk Park** west of Limerick, 9.30am-5.30pm daily, June-Aug 9.30am-7pm – Tel: (061) 361511. **Craggaunowen Project** Mar-Oct 10am-6pm – Tel: (061) 367178. **Aillwee Caves** south of Ballyvaughan, summer 10am-7pm, winter 10am-5pm – Tel: (065) 77036. **Thoor Ballylee** northeast of Gort, open Mar-Oct – Tel: (091) 31436. **Coole Park** grounds north of Gort, daily, all year round.

Bunratty Folk Park

> **❝** *I, the poet William Yeats*
> *With old millboards and*
> *sea-green slates*
> *And smithy work from*
> *the Gort forge*
> *Restored this tower for*
> *my wife George.* **❞**

Craggaunowen Project

Thoor Ballylee

Aillwee Caves

Cliffs of Moher

Galway Food for Thought

Singing pubs, bookshops, theatres and oysters provide sustenance for mind and body in Ireland's fastest-growing city.

● Try the Quay's Bar, and Tigh Neachtain opposite, both in Quay St.

● The September Galway International Oyster Festival is worth waiting for, but at any time of year, this is the place for oysters and a Guinness.

ADDRESS **City maps, Festival & other local information** from the Tourist Office, Aras Fáilte, Victoria Place – Tel: (091) 63081.

St Nicholas Church

Claddagh Ring

● When Galway was Norman, Claddagh village, across Wolfe Tone Bridge, was Irish. It gave its name to the historic Claddagh ring, which is still popular today. See it in jewellers' windows.

ADDRESS **Collegiate Church of St Nicholas** Lombard St, Galway.

The River Corrib

Galway, capital of the province of Connacht, is built on the banks and islands of this rushing, salmon-rich river.

● Take the river walks past the old mill sluices right in the heart of the city.

● In spring, stand on the Salmon Weir Bridge to watch sport anglers and their prey, the leaping silver salmon.

ADDRESS **City maps, Festival & other local information** Galway Tourist Office, Aras Fáilte, Victoria Place – Tel: (091) 63081.

Oyster Festival, Galway

Norman Conquest

'Neither O nor Mac shall strutte ne swagger thro' the streets of Galway' - thus ran an Anglo-Norman by-law. The city grew as an Anglo-Norman settlement surrounded by the 'mere Irish', who were only permitted entry during the day. They came uninvited, though, on raids.

● View the Norman church of St Nicholas of Myra, the largest medieval church in Ireland, with its unique triple nave.

Ship symbol of Galway, Spanish Arch

Lynch's Castle

. The Spanish Connection

Trade and shipwrecked sailors from the Armada forged links between Iberia and Galway, found today in the locals' brown eyes and olive skins.

- Note the Spanish Renaissance Browne Doorway, plus the old port's Spanish Arch. Watch for houses built round open courtyards.

- A Lynch of Lynch's Castle reputedly hanged his son for killing a Spaniard. See his memorial on the wall of the Old Jail behind St Nicholas.

ADDRESSES **The Browne Doorway** now re-erected in Eyre Square, Galway. **Lynch's Castle** now the AIB Bank, Market St, Galway.

Spanish Arch

Salmon Weir Bridge

Glimpses of Clifden

The capital of Connemara, Clifden nestles by the rushing River Owenglin, the twin spires of its Catholic and Protestant churches overseeing its broad streets. Romantic against the eastern sky, the Twelve Pins mountains complete Clifden's picturesque setting.

Clifden

- At Kylemore, pose for the camera near the Benedictine Abbey (1866) – everyone does. Stop for tea. And buns.

- Follow a nature trail in breathtaking 5,000-acre Connemara National Park and cool your feet in a cascade.

- Visit a Norwegian-like fjord at Killary Harbour, one of the finest Connemara inlets, some ten miles long.

- Clifden was the first land-fall for the trans-Atlantic aviators Alcock and Brown. See the limestone sculpture that marks their 1919 touchdown.

ADDRESSES **Alcock & Brown Memorial** signposted, four miles south of Clifden. **Kylemore Abbey** Letterfrack, Feb-Nov, 10am-6pm, tea rooms – Tel: (095) 41113. **Connemara National Park** Visitor Centre Apr-Oct – Tel: (095) 41054.

Connemara National Park

Alcock and Brown Monument

AUTHOR'S TIP

Hire a cycle, head east and follow the circle of lakes – Ballynahinch, Derryclare, Inagh, Kylemore – around the Twelve Pins.

Twelve Pins mountains

Killary Harbour

STALLIONS FROM SPAIN

*C*onnemara became home for Arabian stallions who swam ashore from the shipwrecks of the Spanish Armada. They gave today's Connemara pony large eyes and great agility. Watch for their descendants running wild on the mountainside.

Kylemore Abbey

Aran Islands Options

Once isolated by treacherous seas, though now well served by ferries, these islands have an undeniable romance for those not obliged to winter there.

- Dún Aengus, the cliff-edge fort on Aran's Inishmore, has a cold magic echoed by its three lesser brothers. Once seen, never forgotten.

- Tarred canvas over thin laths in a shape evolved over centuries make currachs still the best choice for inshore fishing. See them in the harbour and watch for them offshore.

Galway hooker

Three men and a currach, Aran Islands

- Galway Hookers, once almost lost, now revived, were the pack-horses of the inter-island stormy seas.

- Robert Flaherty's evocative 1934 film, the classic *Man of Aran*, can still be seen in Kilronan, Inishmore.

GETTING THERE **Boats from Spiddal** – Tel: (099) 61266, **Rossaveal** – Tel: (091) 68903, **Galway** – Tel: (091) 62141 & **Doolin**, Co. Clare, spring to autumn. **Aer Arann** flies from Galway – Tel: (091) 55437. *Man of Aran* **film** Halla Rónáin, Kilronan, summer 3.30 & 7.30pm.

Dún Aengus, Inishmore Island

Island Retreats

Though the Aran Islands are the most visited, Mayo's isles of Inishbofin, Clare and Achill, and Donegal's Aranmore and Tory Islands are not to be missed.

- Grace O'Malley, pirate of the west, saw Elizabeth I as her equal. Her castle stands on Cliara, Clare Island.

- Watch basking sharks in Dooagh Bay, Achill, the largest island off the Irish coast. As other sharks know, deep-sea fishing is good here.

- The Tory Island school of naive painters is best represented by James Dixon's work, much of which hangs in mainland Glebe House.

GETTING THERE **For Inishbofin** from Cleggan – Tel: (095) 45806; **for Clare** from Roonagh Quay, Louisburg – Tel: (098) 26307; **for Achill** drive over the bridge; **for Aranmore** from Burtonport; **for Tory** from Bunbeg or Dunfanaghy. **The Glebe House** Glenveagh, May-Sept 11am-6.30pm, Sundays 1-6.30pm – Tel: (074) 37071.

Inishbofin

Naive art by James Dixon

Grace O'Malley's Castle, Clare Island

Achill Island

Ashford Castle Hotel

Westport Style

In times of privilege, this County Mayo town was elegantly laid out to complement the Marquess of Sligo's 18th-century Westport House.

● Walk beneath lime trees along The Mall where the famed architect James Wyatt canalised the Carrowbeg River.

● Wyatt's dining room in Westport House is the most elegant in Ireland. Rubens' *Holy Family* delights too.

ADDRESSES **Westport House & Gardens** May 2-5pm; June 2-6pm; July & August 10.30am-6 pm, Sun 2-6pm; Sept. 2-5pm house only – Tel: (098) 25430. **Westport Tourist Office** The Mall – Tel: (098) 25711.

Seascapes and Pilgrims

The English novelist William Thackeray voted the view of Clew Bay from around Westport the world's most exquisite. On a clear day, it's hard to disagree.

● Check it out from Westport or Newport quays, or from a boat whilst catching monkfish, ray and conger.

Westport House

The Mall, Westport

Clew Bay from Croagh Patrick's summit

Croagh Patrick, nightfall

- Conical Croagh Patrick (2513ft/764m) dominates the western skyline. Barefooted, pilgrims reach the top of this holy mountain – so can you!

- See Ashford Castle Hotel, beside the ruins of Cong Abbey, near where much of *The Quiet Man* was filmed.

ADDRESSES **Ashford Castle Hotel** Cong – Tel: (092) 46003. **'Lady Betty's' Plaque** the Old Jailhouse, Roscommon, Roscommon Heritage Trail – Tel: (078) 33380.

'LADY BETTY'

*D*estined to be hung for filicide, 'Lady Betty' readily replaced the sick hangman, took to the job with grisly enthusiasm and strung up Roscommon's 18th-century condemned outside her window for thirty years.

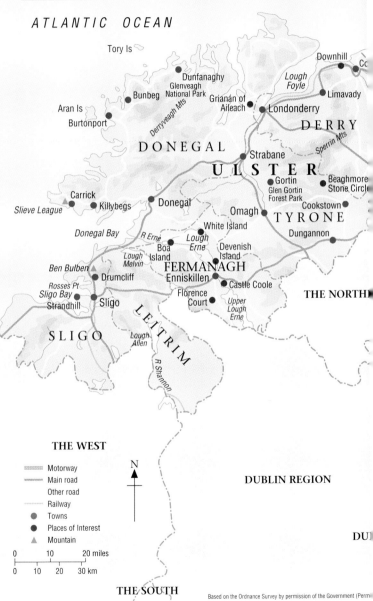

ATLANTIC OCEAN

Tory Is

Downhill
Co

Dunfanaghy
Glenveagh
National Park
Bunbeg
Aran Is
Burtonport

Lough
Foyle
Limavady

Grianán of
Aileach
Londonderry

DERRY

Derryveagh Mts

DONEGAL

Strabane

ULSTER

Sperrin Mts

Gortin
Glen Gortin
Forest Park

Beaghmore
Stone Circle

Carrick
Slieve League
Killybegs
Donegal

Omagh
Cookstown

TYRONE

Donegal Bay

R Erne
Lough
Erne
White Island

Dungannon

Boa
Island
Lough
Melvin
Devenish
Island

Ben Bulben
Drumcliff
FERMANAGH
Enniskillen
Castle Coole

THE NORTH

Rosses Pt
Sligo Bay
Florence
Court
Strandhill
Sligo
Upper
Lough
Erne

SLIGO
LEITRIM
Lough
Allen

R Shannon

THE WEST

N

DUBLIN REGION

Motorway
Main road
Other road
Railway
Towns
Places of Interest
Mountain

DU

0   10   20 miles
0   10   20   30 km

THE SOUTH
Based on the Ordnance Survey by permission of the Government (Permi

THE
NORTHWEST

Sligo's bay is rich in mussels, cockles, native oysters and little clams, and the county's farmland is fertile. The hills at Carrowmore are scattered with megaliths, at Glencar they sweep down to spectacular lakes. 'Peace comes dropping slow' wrote Ireland's most famous poet W.B. Yeats, who found his inspiration here.

Further inland the glens lead to the flatlands of Leitrim and the valley of the River Erne. Set amid the river's great twin lakes are myriad islands, where statues to the old gods lie hidden in the grass amongst the stone towers the Christians built to secure their treasures from the dreaded Vikings. Far from Dublin and Belfast, the big estates of later English settlers survived till death duties led the way for some into the welcoming embrace of the National Trust.

North of Fermanagh, Tyrone – finally settled by imported Scots – reflects a different history. There are few towns in Tyrone, and beyond them the independent nature of those settlers who lasted the course is reflected in self-contained small farms, each with its buildings shielded by ash and sycamore, each with a long and winding lane connecting it to the county road. After a time many Ulster-Scots settlers found the English promises hollow and left for the Americas, taking with them their independence and the birth of the American Dream. A dozen U.S. presidents' ancestral homesteads are hereabouts.

Wild Donegal's people had less choice. What little good land there was in the valleys had to be shared between an increasing number of inheritors. The abandoned potato ridges and the miles of painstakingly built stone walls are often the only evidence of lost settlements. The Gaelic language, overheard frequently in the shops of Galway city, survives, with State support, in special Gaeltacht areas.

Compared to the rest of Ireland, the Northwest is the probably the least-developed tourist destination – and is all the better for it. Here peace still does come dropping slow along some of the most unspoilt shorelines of sea and lake anywhere in Europe. Grasp the moment.

Isle of Inisfree

Sligo Spells

W.B. Yeats set the style by holidaying here early in the century. Many shopfronts have barely altered since.

Jack Yeats' self portrait in Sligo Art Gallery

- W.B's brother, Jack, was one of Ireland's finest painters. Sligo's galleries and museums lovingly record both brothers' skills.

- See Yeats' statue in Sligo town square and his tombstone in the quiet churchyard at Drumcliff.

- Stop to see the souvenirs of the remarkable Countess Markievicz that adorn her beloved Lissadell House near Drumcliff. A friend of Yeats and a heroine of the 1916 Rising, she was the first woman elected to Westminster.

- Table-top mountain Ben Bulben has a special place in Irish mythology, but there's an easier climb up Strandhill's Knocknarea for a grand view.

- At the resort of Rosses Point note the Metal Man sea channel marker that Yeats dubbed 'the Rosses Point man who never told a lie'. Pause to enjoy the fine golf-links.

ADDRESSES Sligo County Library complex on Stephen St includes **Municipal Art Gallery** Tue-Fr 10.30am-12.30pm, **Sligo County Museum & Yeats Memorial Museum** 10.30am-12.30pm & 2.30-4.30pm. **Lissadell House** May-Sept Mon-Sat 2-5.15pm.

Lissadell House

> **66** *Cast a cold Eye
> On Life, on Death.
> Horseman, pass by!* **99**

Ben Bulben

White Island figures

Fermanagh's Lakeland

Mysterious pagan heads and great Anglo-Irish houses look down on the two island-dotted loughs of the lakeland.

- By Ceithleann's Island, Enniskillen, see Wyatt's Georgian Castle Coole and the rococo Florence Court.

- Tea in Florence Court should follow 'mission underground' by boat through nearby Marble Arch Caves.

- Devenish's tower protected Christianity from the Vikings, but who knows what dark practices Boa and White Islands' figures first defended.... See them to speculate.

ADDRESSES National Trust's **Castle Coole** June Fr-Mon, July-Aug Wed-Mon, Sept Sat-Sun all 2-6pm and **Florence Court** Apr-Sept Wed-Mon noon-6pm. **Devenish ferry** Apr-Sept Tue-Sat 10am-7pm, Sun 2-7pm from Trory – Tel: (0365) 22711. **White Island** ferry from Castle Archdale, June-Aug Tue-Sat 10am-7pm, Sun 2-7pm. **Boa Island** is reached by road. **Marble Arch Caves** June, Sept, Oct Mon-Sat 11am-4.30pm, Sun 11am-5pm; July-Aug Mon-Sat 11am-5pm, Sun 11am-6pm – Tel: (0365) 82777.

Wall fountain, Florence Court

Marble Arch Caves

Donegal – the Door West

Whereas Sligo is the southwest's gateway to the north, Donegal town is its door to Derry, and the north's door west.

- See Basil Brooke's fine Jacobean castle in Donegal town centre.

- See too Glenveagh Castle in Glenveagh National Park.

- Fishing, which once helped farmers survive, has Killybegs bustling still.

- A half'un in Carrick's Slieve League bar is best taken after – not before – a look over the nearby sea cliffs....

- Wrap up against the Atlantic's mists in hand-woven Donegal tweed. It's renowned worldwide for its quality.

ADDRESSES Maps from Donegal Tourist Office, The Quay – Tel: (073) 21148. **Glenveagh National Park** Visitor Centre Easter-Oct daily – Tel: (074) 37090.

Tweed loom

Killybegs fishermen

Slieve League

Ulster-American Folk Park

An American Tale

Denied public office, denied markets, denied religious freedom, 250,000 Nonconformist Ulster-Scots planters left Ireland in the 18th century. They sailed the Atlantic and helped create America.

- At Camphill, County Tyrone, the Ulster-American Folk Park recreates the cottages they left, the ships they sailed, and the landfalls they made.

- A Wilson left a modest farm at Dergalt – now the Wilson Homestead – and sailed for America. His tenth son's son, Woodrow, was the tenth U.S. President to hail from the region.

- Meet Sika deer and wildfowl at Omagh's Gortin Glen Forest Park.

- Omagh's Ulster History Park displays Ireland's dwelling places, from the first wattle-and-hide shelters.

ADDRESSES **Ulster-American Folk Park** Camphill, Omagh, Easter-Sept Mon-Sat 11am-6pm, Sun 11.30am-6.30pm; winter Mon-Fr 10.30am-4.30pm – Tel: (0662) 243292. **The Wilson Homestead** Dergalt, Strabane, Apr-Sept daily ex Sun, Thur and public hols 2-5.30pm or by appt – Tel: (0504) 243292. **Gortin Glen Forest Park** all year, daily, 10am-sunset – Tel: (06626) 48217. **Ulster History Park** Gortin Glen Forest Park, Easter-Sept Mon-Fr 11am-6pm, Sat 11am-7pm, Sun 1-7pm; Oct-Mar daily 11am-5pm – Tel: (06626) 48188.

Gortin Glen Forest Park

HISTORIC HOMES

*D*eep in Gortin Glen Forest Park, the Ulster History Park has on display fascinating replicas of Ireland's dwelling places, from the first wattle-and-hide shelters to homes of the 17th century.

The Maiden City

Derry's position on a hill overlooking the River Foyle gave it a strategic potential too big to be left in the hands of ordinary folk. From the Vikings that attacked St Columb's first abbey in 546, invaders have come and gone. The many sieges the town withstood gave it its nickname.

● Impregnable since 1613, the mile-long city walls are amongst the most complete in Europe.

● See the shellcase that contained the encircling Catholic army's terms of capitulation during the great seige of 1689 in St Columb's Cathedral. Protestant Londonderry's reply – 'No Surrender' – is still heard in the city.

● Cahir O'Doherty razed and pillaged Derry in 1608. A new stone tower and a genealogical centre commemorates his (and your?) clan.

ADDRESSES **Maps of the walls** Tourist Office, near the Guildhall – Tel: (0504) 267284. **St Columb's Cathedral** 9am-1pm, 2-5pm – Tel: (0504) 262746. **O'Doherty Tower** Magazine St, Mon-Fr 9am-5pm – Tel: (0504) 269792.

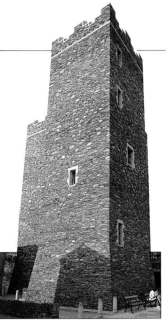
O'Doherty's Tower

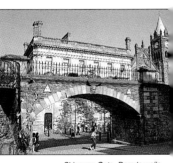
Shipquay Gate, Derry's walls

Derry's walls, St Columb's Cathedral

Beyond the Maiden

Inside the city's walls the medieval road plan survives and Georgian buildings dot the streets. Outside, the rich Foyle delta awaits you.

- Frederick Augustus Hervey, the Earl Bishop, built a memorial temple for his young cousin, Mrs Mussenden, in the loveliest spot he could find.

- The Greek geographer Ptolemy recorded the Grianán of Aileach (1700 BC). This vast, complex stone fort was once the royal seat of the O'Neills, early kings of Ulster.

- Sense the atmosphere at Beaghmore's stone circles. It's only the wind (you hope) crying under the wide sky....

ADDRESSES **Mussenden Temple** Downhill, Apr-Sept 12-6pm National Trust – Tel: (02657) 32143. **Grianán of Aileach** south of Fahan, west of Derry. **Beaghmore Stone Circles** Dunnamore, northeast of Cookstown. Both sites are open all year.

Mussenden Temple

Beaghmore Stone Circles

Grianán of Aileach

ATLANTIC
OCEAN

NORTH CHANNEL

Giant's
Causeway
Carrick-
a-Rede
Bushmills
Ballycastle

Mts of
Antrim

R Bann

Ballymena
Larne

ANTRIM

Carrickfergus
Bangor

ULSTER

Lough
Neagh
Belfast
Cultra
Donaghadee
Mount Stewart H
Lisburn
Castle
Espie
Greyabbey
Strangford
Lough

THE NORTHWEST

The
Argory
Hillsborough

R Bann

Armagh
Portaferry

Navan
Fort
DOWN
Downpatrick

Monaghan
ARMAGH
Legananny
Dolmen

Clones
Newry

MONAGHAN
Mourne
Mts

IRISH
SEA

THE
NORTH-
WEST

Carrickmacross

DUBLIN REGION

N

	Motorway
	Main road
	Other road
	Railway
●	Towns
●	Places of Interest
▲	Mountain

0   10   20 mile

0   10   20   30 km

DUBLIN

Based on the Ordnance Survey by permission of the Government (Permit No. 5633)

—54—

THE NORTHEAST

W hilst the old Celtic warlords held out in the northwest for longer than anywhere else, the Anglo-Normans built a string of strong castles along the northeast coast. Slowly, against many reverses, English colonists and their Scots planters won the land east of the two River Banns, which, with Lough Neagh, divides the now separate British province of Northern Ireland diagonally in two. Indeed Scotland was never far away. You can see it from many a spot along the Down and Antrim coasts. Raiding and trading split and united families. Rathlin was proved Irish only from its absence of snakes, St Patrick having banished them from all of Ireland. The Giant's Causeway, legend has it, was just a set of giant's stepping stones from the north coast to Scotland. Visit the pubs and browse the fair-day markets and you'll find Antrim's accents close to Ayrshire's.

One hundred years ago this was a land peopled by weavers. The green fields were given over to growing and bleaching flax. Now the patchwork fields are held in smallholdings of a few acres of grass, barley, oats or potatoes. Many of them are let out, the owners finding work, if they can, in the light industries of neighbouring towns. Most of the once great linen mills are now silent, but Belfast's still great shipyards are fighting back against foreign competition. Here and there, in the country, between neat thorn hedges, old water mills crumble beside rushing streams.

The rich fields of Down were always fertile. The county has over 1,300 early Christian circular raths, each denoting a farmstead. In Armagh, the orchards, town plans and manor houses speak more of England than Ireland. In the neat towns of all three counties, churches of all denominations cluster together near 'The Diamond' – 'a Diamond as big as a Square' – where, always, a monument recalls Ulster's fallen in the First World War.

Despite their 'Troubles', the peoples of Ulster's two communities preserve a shared wry humour, a shared welcome for strangers and a shared desire to tell you how, really, life for them goes on as normal.

Mountains of Mourne

Antrim Alternatives

Only thirteen miles from Scotland, County Antrim borders the largest lake in the British Isles and boasts a magnificent coastline, great for touring.

● Take the Antrim Coast Road for mighty cliffs and views of Scotland.

● Along the way, turn off to visit one of Antrim's beautiful Nine Glens.

● Test your nerves on the rope bridge over a sea-chasm at Carrick-a-Rede – it looks more frightening than it is.

Carrick-a-Rede rope bridge

Antrim glens

Bushmills Distillery

● Make sure you don't miss the strangely perfect hexagonals of the Giant's Causeway.

● Warm up afterwards at the historic Bushmills Distillery, where they've made great whiskey since 1609.

ADDRESSES **Carrick-a-Rede rope bridge** Ballintoy, May-Sept National Trust – Tel: (02657) 32143. **Bushmills Distillery** Bushmills, Mon-Thu, tours 10.30am and 2.30pm, Fr 10.30am only – Tel: (02657) 31521.

Belfast Bounty

The city, Ireland's youngest, was only a series of forts until Huguenot refugees streamlined linen production in the 17th century. Shipbuilding and ropemaking came later. Together, they made Belfast.

Giant's Causeway

Linen Hall Library, Belfast

- The Linen Hall Library presents an 18th-century oasis of calm amid Belfast's bustle.

- Take local oysters and a Guinness in the Crown Liquor Saloon snug, and marvel at a bar as ornately Victorian as the Opera House opposite.

- Spain's Armada, wrecked on Ireland's shores, left golden artefacts, copied for sale in the city's Ulster Museum.

ADDRESSES **Northern Ireland Tourist Board** St Anne's Court, North St – Tel: (0232) 246609. **Linen Hall Library** (with cafe), 17 Donegall Sq Nth, open till 6pm weekdays, 4pm Sat – Tel: (0232) 321707. **Crown Liquor Saloon** 46 Great Victoria S, Mon-Sat 11.30am-11pm, Sun 12.30-2.30pm & 7-10pm – Tel: (0232) 249476. **Ulster Museum** Stranmillis Rd, Mon-Fr 10am-5pm, Sat 1-5pm, Sun 2-5pm – Tel: (0232) 320202.

Crown Liquor Saloon, Belfast

The Belfast Triangle

Three towns mark the limits of the city's commuter dormitories – Bangor, Lisburn and Carrickfergus – known to the locals as the Belfast Triangle.

- The superb Ulster Folk and Transport Museum's acres hold evocative cottages and streets of yesteryear.

- Carrickfergus' castle awaits lovers of ramparts and parapets – considered the finest in Ireland.

ADDRESSES **Ulster Folk & Transport Museum** Cultra, Mon-Sat 10.30am-6pm, Sun 2-6pm, winter museum closes 4.30pm – Tel: (0232) 428428. **Carrickfergus Castle** Carrickfergus, Mon-Sat 10am-6pm, Sun 2-6pm – Tel: (09603) 51273.

Ulster Folk and Transport Museum

Carrickfergus Castle

The Ards of Down

Whitewashed windmills and gateposts served as landmarks for the fishermen-farmers of this hilly county.

- Only two windmills still work in all Ireland. Visit Ballycopeland's for an idea of how things used to be.

- Strangford Lough is home for wintering birds, grey seals and 2,000 marine species, most of which can be seen in Portaferry's aquarium.

- See the tombs of the Montgomery family and the fine West doorway among the ruins of Greyabbey, once a Cistercian monastery.

Greyabbey

Mount Stewart House

- Take a day to see the magnificent gardens of Mount Stewart House – there's a tea shop for the thirsty.

ADDRESSES **Ballycopeland Windmill** Donaghadee, Apr-Sept Tue-Sat 10am-7pm, Sun 2-7pm; Oct-Mar Sat 10am-4pm, Sun 2-4pm. **Grace Neill's Inn** High St, Donaghadee, Mon-Sat 11.30am-11pm – Tel: (0247) 882553. **Portaferry Aquarium** Apr-Aug Tue-Sat 10am-8pm, Sun 1-8pm; Sept-Mar Tue-Sat 10.30am-5pm, Sun 1-5pm. **Castle Espie Wetlands Centre** (birds) Mar-Oct Wed-Sat 10.30am-5.30pm; July-Aug also Sun 2-6pm; Nov-Feb Sat only – Tel: (0247) 874146. **Greyabbey** Easter-Sept Tue-

IRELAND'S OLDEST INN

*B*oswell, Keats, Liszt, Wordsworth, Peter the Great and Brendan Behan entered Donaghadee's harbour and supped in the country's oldest inn, Grace Neill's. Sense the history here.

Ballycopeland Windmill

Sat 10am-7pm; Sun 2-7pm; Oct-Mar Sat 10am-4pm, Sun 2-4pm. **Mount Stewart House & Garden** National Trust, Newtownards, Easter daily 1-6pm; Apr-May & Sept-Oct Sat, Sun & Bank Hol only 1-6pm; June-Aug daily ex Tue noon-6pm – Tel: (024774) 387.

Kingdom of Mourne

Castles command every hilltop, yet before they did, St Patrick, Ireland's special saint, landed to preach the Word.

- See St Patrick's grave in Downpatrick Cathedral churchyard.

- Ulster's hero, Cuchulainn, fought at Navan Fort, near enchanting Georgian Armagh, and blonde Queen Macha built an Irish Camelot there. Climb it for the great view.

Don't venture home without some distinctive Monaghan lace from Carrickmacross or Clones.

- Set high on the hill known as Cratlieve near Dromara, Legananny is a classic dolmen in a scholar's eyes. It appears in the legends of this region, though, as a giant's grave.

- Stand still with time at The Argory, a mansion where the gas lamps are lit, the table laid for dinner and the cues polished for billiards….

ADDRESSES **Down Cathedral** open till 6pm, pilgrimage 17th Mar – Tel: (0396) 841311. **Navan Fort** and **Legananny Dolmen** always open. **The Argory** Moy, Co. Armagh, National Trust, Apr-May Sat & Sun; June-Aug daily ex Tue; Sept Sat & Sun, all 12-6pm – Tel: (08687) 84753.

St Patrick's Grave

Legananny Dolmen

WALK ON

WALKING IN IRELAND

In answer to a survey, potential French tourists cited a walk in the rain as a prime reason for visiting Ireland. That type of rainy day is described as 'soft' by the Irish, a day when a light drizzle feels gentle on the face, bringing with it the tang of the surrounding sea, a slight chill off the heather-covered granite hills, the scent of peat from the bog, or crushed grass underfoot. But the sun does· shine too, mostly in May and June and perhaps on the wild flowers by the lakes, or on those hidden in the Burren's fissures and by Rathlin Island's rocks.

County Clare walking country

Over 1,000 miles of country walks in Ireland are waymarked with discreet symbols, and they range along abandoned railway tracks, canal banks, old drovers' roads, narrow lanes known as boreens, country parks, riversides, over stone walls and stiles atop gentle hills, running down to sea cliffs and beaches. A combination of Ordnance Survey maps (1 inch = 1 mile is ideal) and the relevant tourist walking literature will provide a vast choice of environments and adventures. Most of the major walks have further supporting literature linking them in with the nearest farmhouse, camp site, private hostel or Youth Hostel Accommodation.

Major way-marked walks, where rights of way have been secured, include the 500-mile Ulster Way, which almost completes a circuit of Northern Ireland and for which you should allow three weeks or so if you wish to finish it. This main route links with three of the thirteen major walks in the South. These include the eighty-two-mile Wicklow Way through the Wicklow Mountains, and the sixteen-mile Cavan Way. St Patrick's Vale, County Down, has St Patrick's Way, while the Burren and the Aran Islands have their own shorter walks.

Ballaghbeama Gap, Macgillycuddy's Reeks

Of course, it's not compulsory to complete a whole Way. With bus and train timetables, lifts arranged from friends and acquaintances old and new, from your country house or hotel, or in tandem with bike hire, or hitchhiking (which works well on country lanes), sections can be made and broken to fit your plans. Be sensible about weather: waterproof boots, cleated soles, raingear and warm clothes for the mornings and evenings are musts at any time of the year.

Don't forget that not all walks are in the country. Town trails, backed by clear maps, are springing up, particularly in the cities, and Dublin even has a guided literary summer pub crawl. Tel: (01) 540228.

Bloody cranesbill, the Burren

Addresses
REPUBLIC OF IRELAND Bord Fáilte has a useful composite all-Ireland walking map/leaflet on the thirteen major walks, including the Ulster Way, plus various individual information sheets. **Maps** Government Publications Sales Office, Sun Alliance Hse, Molesworth St, Dublin 2 – Tel: (01) 710309. **National Sports Council** (Cospóir), Long Distance Walking Routes Committee, Hawkins Hse, Hawkins St,

Long-distance walking route sign

Dublin 2 – Tel: (01) 734700. **An Oige (Irish Youth Hostel Association)** 39 Mountjoy Sq, Dublin 1 – Tel: (01) 363111. The Republic also has a number of other hostels grouped as Independent Hostels and Budget Hostels.

NORTHERN IRELAND Maps Her Majesty's Stationery Office, HMSO, 80 Chichester St, Belfast, BT1 4LE – Tel: (0232) 238451. **Ulster Federation of Rambling Clubs** 27 Slieve Gallion Drive, Belfast, BT11 8JN – Tel: (0232) 624289. Ulster Way leaflets from the **Sports Council of Northern Ireland** House of Sport, Upper Malone Rd, Belfast, BT9 5LA – Tel: (0232) 381222. **Youth Hostel Association of Northern Ireland** 93 Dublin Rd, Belfast, BT2 7HP – Tel: (0232) 324733.

Hiking weather

TIGHT LINES

FISHING IN IRELAND

Around the south and west, the Gulf Stream warms Ireland's coastal waters, but off the northwest lies the cold Atlantic. Even in summer the big rollers can pound the rocky ledges, the mist-shrouded cliffs and the long crescents of silver sand. Thus, from the sport angler's and seafood aficionado's point of view, Ireland's 3,000 miles of coastline provide the best of many worlds. Sea bream may range north from the Mediterranean and from Biscay. Halibut might wander south from Greenland. Where cold and warm currents meet, the waters are rich in plankton, the start of a rich food chain which does everything from fattening fine oysters in the bays of Galway and Sligo to bringing sporting shark and tunny within the range of well-equipped charter boats. The cold water turning round the north coast, over sandy shoals, is favoured by turbot and brill, while the waves crashing on westward-facing beaches toss shellfish in the surf, bringing in school bass.

Sufficient numbers of Ireland's wild salmon escape the miles-long off-shore nets and inshore fixed engines to provide superb sport for the fly fisher when they return to their native rivers to spawn. Spring salmon run 8-12lbs, grilse average 6lbs, while big fish up to 30lbs are taken in summer. Thunder & Lightning and Black

Salmon, River Moy, County Mayo

Goldfinch are popular fly patterns. Sea trout, a summer fish, are having difficult times in recent years; in the West you will find vigorous protesters blaming their decline on a rise in sea lice generated, allegedly, by commercial salmon farming.

Brown trout, widely available in beer-brown streams, grow fastest in the limestone lakes of the central plains – Ennel, Owel, Sheelin and Erne – and can also grow to enormous sizes in the big lakes such as Erne and Corrib. Lough Melvin has three genetically unique trout species, the sonaghan, gillaroo and ferox, as well as brownies and charr.

Pike lurk in the reed beds of Ireland's lakes. Look at a map and see what percentage of the island is lake, river and stream. What the French refer to as white fish, the English as coarse fish – roach, rudd, bream and perch – are everywhere. Carp and tench are found in specific swims, dace in the Cork Blackwater. In all, over 150 species of edible, sporting fish may be taken in Irish waters, salt and fresh.

No licences or permits are required for sea angling north or south of the Border,

River Blackwater, County Cork

Bass fishing, Dingle Bay

Local regulations covering methods of fishing, bag limit, seasons etc. will be available from tackle shops, tourist offices and club secretaries when applying for licences.

In general, game fishing runs from early spring to late autumn. There is no close season for pike or coarse (white) fish.

Further details of angling in the areas covered by the eight Regional Fisheries Boards in the Republic and the corresponding authorities in Northern Ireland can be obtained from the respective tourist boards. Hookline, a telephone information service, is available on (01) 618172.

except in estuaries, where a licence for scarce sea trout is required. Otherwise weather is the only constraint. There is no close season, but, on occasions, certain species may have conservation orders.

Throughout Ireland a licence is necessary for salmon fishing. Permits to fish salmon rivers are also required. In the Republic, anglers under eighteen and over sixty-six do not need a rod licence to fish for brown trout, rainbow trout and coarse fish. Permission by permit is required.

In Northern Ireland neither anglers under eighteen fishing for coarse fish exclusively, nor anglers of any age fishing in the Foyle area just for coarse fish need any licence. A permit to fish, from State, club or riparian owner is always necessary. Trout anglers always need a rod licence.

Fishermen – this way!

Salmon, River Laune, County Kerry

A River Liffey catch, County Kildare

ISLAND OF GREENS

GOLFING IN IRELAND

A 4,000-hole golf course with towns and villages scattered in between – this is Ireland.

There are almost 300 golf courses in Ireland, over 200 of which are in the Republic. In general, green fees are less than in most golfing countries, and courses less crowded. Visitors are given a typical Irish welcome in the great majority of clubs and it is only at weekends in high season that the traveller will find it hard to to get a round. Nevertheless, it is advisable to avoid disappointment by telephoning ahead.

Though there are a great number of beautifully situated parkland courses, many in attractive lake and riverside settings, the real challenge for the golfer lies in the magnificent links courses strung along the coastline. Here the combination of sand dunes and gravelly soils interspersed with gorse bushes, mists and sea-sculpted rock formations creates great natural courses.

Lahinch Golf Club, County Clare

There is a particular spring to the naturally drained turf and, to a golfer, fierce hazards, such as the natural squalls and the buffeting of the wind off the sea. Bring a lightweight waterproof suit and reduce your number of clubs. Electric carts are few and far between – pull-buggies and caddies are plentiful and essential.

The following is a selection of the famed courses:

● Royal Dublin, just outside the city, was built in 1885 on a man-made island. The Irish Open is held here. North Bull Island – Tel: (01) 336346.

● Portmarnock, described by Arnold Palmer as the world's finest natural golf course, was the venue for the first Irish Open in 1889, won by the appropriately named John Ball. The course record of 66 is shared by Gary Player and Christy O'Connor. North County Dublin – Tel: (01) 323082.

● Its first originally designed by Henry Longhurst, the Killarney Golf and Fishing Club now has two courses in the lee of Macgillycuddy's Reeks. There are stories of balls at the 19th hole bouncing off trout in Lough Leane – Tel: (064) 31034.

● Rosses Point in County Sligo is the home of the West of Ireland Amateur Championship – Tel: (071) 77134.

View from Killarney's clubhouse

Royal Dublin

Portmarnock, County Dublin

- Kerry's Waterville, an American-style course, attracts the Bob Hopes and Sean Connerys – Tel: (066) 74102.

- Tralee's course, between river, sea and crumbling castles at Ardfert, Tralee, was Arnold Palmer's first design in Europe. He calls it the world's greatest. The 12th and 13th holes are legendary – Tel: (066) 36379.

- Ballybunion's Old Course, also in County Kerry, was used by Tom Watson to toughen up for the British Open. Tom reckoned the par 4, 446-yard 11th hole to be the toughest in the world – Tel: (068) 27146.

- Clare's Lahinch was built for the Black Watch Regiment. A note on the no-hands barometer advises 'See goats'. They disappear, anticipating bad weather. Tom Morris designed the Old Course's eccentric blind holes in 1893 – Tel: (065) 81003.

Royal County Down, Newcastle

- Royal Portrush in County Antrim, and Newcastle's Royal County Down are both listed, like Ballybunion, in the top dozen in the world by the World Golf Writers' Association. The 217-yard, par 3 14th, 'Calamity', at Portrush is almost as famous as the tiny on-course bar at another hole – Tel: Portrush (0265) 822311, Newcastle (03967) 22209.

ADDRESSES **Golfing Union of Ireland** (covers NI as well) Glencar House, 81 Eglinton Rd, Donnybrook, Dublin 4 – Tel: (01) 2694111. **Irish Ladies Golf Union** 1 Clonskeagh Sq, Clonskeagh Rd, Dublin 14 – Tel: (01) 2696244; Northern Ireland branch 58a High St, Holywood, Co. Down – Tel: (02317) 3708.

Waterville, Kerry

ANNUAL EVENTS

January
- Five Nations Rugby Internationals begin, Lansdowne Rd, Dublin – Tel: (01) 684601.

February
- Rugby Internationals continue.
- Ulster Harp National Steeplechase, Downpatrick, Co. Down, mid-month – Tel: (0396) 612054.
- Dublin Film Festival, end of month – Tel: (01) 679 2937.

St Patrick's Day Parade, Dublin

March
- St Patrick's Day, 17th, parade in Dublin; celebrations at St Patrick's burial place, Downpatrick/Saul, Co. Down – Tel: (0396) 841311.
- 17th, Horse Ploughing Match, Ballycastle, Co. Antrim – Tel: (026 67) 62024
- International Set-Dancing, Galway city, late March – Tel: (091) 21981.

Traditional dancing

April
- Irish Grand National, Fairyhouse, Co. Meath, Easter – Tel: (01) 289 7277.
- Mullingar International Coarse Fishing Festival, Co. Westmeath, end of the month – Tel: (044) 40431.
- Punchestown Irish National Hunt Festival, Co. Kildare, end of the month – Tel: (01) 289 7277.

May
- Cork International Choral Festival (end April/early May), Cork city – Tel: (021) 312296.
- North West 200, fastest motorcycle road race in British Isles, Portstewart, Co. Derry, mid-month – Tel: (0232) 246609.
- An Flea Nua, a festival of traditional Irish music, Ennis, Co. Clare – Tel: (065) 28366.

June
- Festival of Music in Great Irish Houses – Tel: (01) 962021.
- Castleward Opera, Co. Down, Ireland's Glyndebourne – Tel: (0396) 86204.
- Bloomsday, 16th, Sandycove, Co. Dublin – Tel: (01) 747733.
- Budweiser Irish Derby, The Curragh, Co. Kildare – Tel: (01) 289 7277.
- Fiddle Stone Festival, Beleek, Co. Fermanagh – Tel: (0365) 323110.
- Nun Run, Trim Pony Races, Trim, Co. Meath, late June – Tel: (046) 31813.

July
- Siamsa na Gaillimhe, Galway's Folk Theatre, Galway town – Tel: (091) 55479.
- Cobh International Folk Dance Festival, Co. Cork – Tel: (021) 813301.
- Galway Arts Festival, international status, Galway town – Tel: (091) 63800.

Kerrygold Dublin Horse Show

- Galway Races, Galway city, late July or early August – Tel: (01) 289 7077.

August
- Ballyshannon International Folk & Traditional Music Festival, Co. Donegal, early August – Tel: (072) 51049.
- Kerrygold Dublin Horse Show, RDS Showgrounds, Dublin – Tel: (01) 680645.
- Kilkenny Arts Week, Co. Kilkenny, mid-month, classical music – Tel: (056) 61497.
- Yeats International Summer School, Sligo town – Tel: (071) 61201.
- Connemara Pony Show, Clifden, Co. Galway, third Thur – Tel: (095) 21863.
- Rose of Tralee Festival, Co. Kerry, third week – Tel: (066) 31322.

September
- Clarenbridge Oyster Festival, Co. Galway, 2nd weekend – Tel: (091) 96001.
- Waterford International Festival of Light Opera, Waterford town, third/fourth week – Tel: (051) 75437.

Connemara Pony Show

Hurling Final

- All Ireland Hurling Finals, 1st Sun, All Ireland Gaelic Football Finals, 3rd Sun, both at Croke Park, Dublin – Tel: (01) 747733.
- Galway International Oyster Festival, Co. Galway, last weekend – Tel: (091) 22066.

October
- Dublin Theatre Festival, early Oct – Tel: (01) 778439.
- International Gourmet Festival, Kinsale, Co. Cork, first weekend – Tel: (021) 774026.
- Cork International Film Festival, Cork city, second week – Tel: (021) 271711.
- Wexford Opera Festival, Wexford town, last week/first week Nov – Tel: (053) 22144.
- Guinness Cork Jazz Festival, Cork city, last weekend – Tel: (021) 545411.

November
- Belfast Festival at Queen's University, arts festival second only to Edinburgh's in the British Isles, last three weeks – Tel: (0232) 667687.

December
- Christmas Racing, Boxing Day, various venues including Leopardstown, Co. Dublin – Tel: (01) 289 7277.

USEFUL INFORMATION

MONEY: The unit of currency in the North is the pound (£) sterling. In the Republic it is the punt (£), written as IR£, which usually stays within a few percent of the value of the pound sterling. It divides into 100 pence. Branches of Irish banks are widespread, and open Mon-Fr 10am-12.30pm & 1.30-3pm, sometimes to 5pm Thur, in the Republic. Lunchtime opening can be expected in city centre branches. In the North, bank hours are 10am-3.30pm Mon-Fr. In tiny villages bank hours may be restricted to a few a week. Credit cards are widely accepted in hotels, restaurants and petrol stations (but in few pubs and only in large stores) in all but the smallest villages. Eurocheque and Travellers Cheques have the same range of acceptance.

INTERNAL TRAVEL: Bringing your own car or car hire is ideal, for though the limited rail (Iarnrod Eireann and NI Railways) and bus (CIE and Ulsterbus mainly) facilities are efficient, services and connections in rural areas are infrequent. Driving is on the left. The speed limit in the Republic is 55mph, in the North 60mph (Motorways 70mph). Signposts give distance in miles in the North, in a confusing mixture of miles and kilometres in the South.

TOURIST BOARDS Bord Fáilte/Irish Tourist Board Baggot St Bridge, Dublin 2 – Tel: (01) 765871. **Northern Ireland Tourist Board** St Anne's Court, 59 North St, Belfast, BT1 INB – Tel: (0232) 246609. **All Ireland Information Bureau** British Travel Centre, 12 Regent St, Piccadilly Circus, London, SW1Y 4QP – Tel: (071) 8398416.

Pub musicians

PUBS The Republic's opening hours are Mon-Sat 10am-11.30pm, Sun 12.30-2.30pm & 4-11.00pm. Winter closing at 11pm every night. In NI the hours are Mon-Sat 11.30am-11pm, Sun 12.30-2.30pm & 7-10pm. Late licences are found in pubs with music, and rural pub owners don't always clockwatch.

PHONES International call prefix 00 in the Republic; 010 in the North. Prefix 08 before the code for calls to Northern Ireland from the Republic.

SECURITY The police are the Garda (plural Gardaí), in the Republic, and the Royal Ulster Constabulary (RUC) in the North. Ordinary crime is low across Ireland, though normal precautions

Jaunting car

Routefinder?

against pickpockets etc. are necessary in big cities. Road checks, manned by the RUC and/or the British Army or the Ulster Defence Regiment (UDR) are a fact of life north of the border. Always cross the border at the official crossing places. As anywhere else in the world, stay cool and polite and everyone else will too. Emergency: – Tel: 999.

EMBASSIES Dublin: **Australia** Fitzwilton Hse, Wilton Terrace – Tel: (01) 761517. **Belgium** Shrewsbury Hse, 2 Shrewsbury Rd – Tel: (01) 692082. **Canada** 65 St Stephen's Green – Tel: (01) 781988. **Denmark** 121 St Stephen's Green – Tel: (01) 756404. **France** 36 Ailesbury Rd – Tel: (01) 694777. **Germany** 31 Trimleston Ave, Blackrock – Tel: (01) 693011. **Greece** 1 Upper

Old-fashioned telephone box

Pembroke St – Tel: (01) 767254/5. **Italy** 63 Northumberland Rd – Tel: (01) 601744. **Japan** 22 Ailesbury Rd – Tel: (01) 694244. **Netherlands** 160 Merrion Row – Tel: (01) 693444. **Norway** Hainault Hse, 69 St Stephen's Green – Tel: (01) 783133. **Portugal** Knocksinna Hse, Knocksinna Park, Foxrock – Tel: (01) 289 4416. **Spain** 17a Merlin Park – Tel: (01) 691640. **Sweden** Sun Alliance Hse, Dawson St – Tel: (01) 715822. **UK** 31 Merrion Rd – Tel: (01) 695211. **USA** 42 Elgin Rd – Tel: (01) 688777.

Where the sun always shines…

CONSULATES Belfast: **Belgium** 29 Lisburn St, Hillsborough – Tel: (0232) 682671. **Denmark & Sweden** 10 Victoria St – Tel: (0232) 230581. **Finland** 14A Lennoxvale – Tel: (0232) 669843. **Germany** 1 Ballyhampton Rd, Larne – Tel: (0574) 260777. **Greece** 72 High St – Tel: (0232) 242242. **Italy** 7 Richmond Park – Tel: (0232) 668854. **Netherlands** 25 Randalstown Rd, Antrim – Tel: (08494) 668854. **Norway** as Greece. **Portugal** as Greece. **USA** Queen's Hse, Queen St – Tel: (0232) 328239.

Index

The publishers would like to thank the following for their assistance:

The Board of Trinity College, Dublin

Trevor Ó Clochartaigh, Taibhdhearc na Gaillimhe

Connie Kelleher, Cork Public Museum

William Gallaher, John Scarry, Office of Public Works, Dublin

R. C. Guinness, Straffan Steam Museum

The staff of the Irish National Stud

Alan McCartney, Ulster Folk and Transport Museum

J. C. McTernan, Sligo County Library

Gabrielle Noble

Catherine Power, The Scarteen Hunt

R. Watson